LEGO

GEAR BOTS

By the Editors of Klutz

KLUTZ

CONTENTS

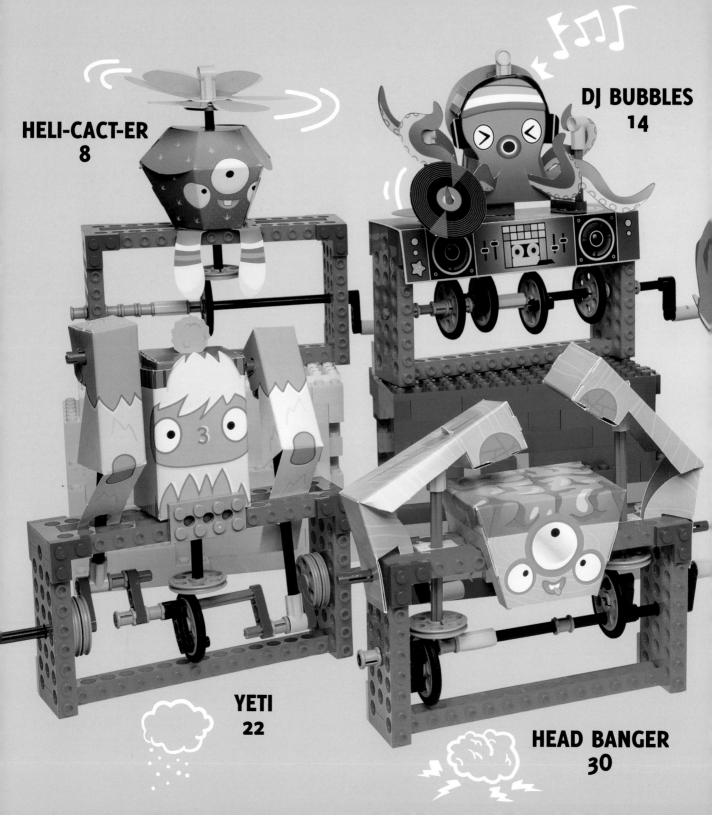

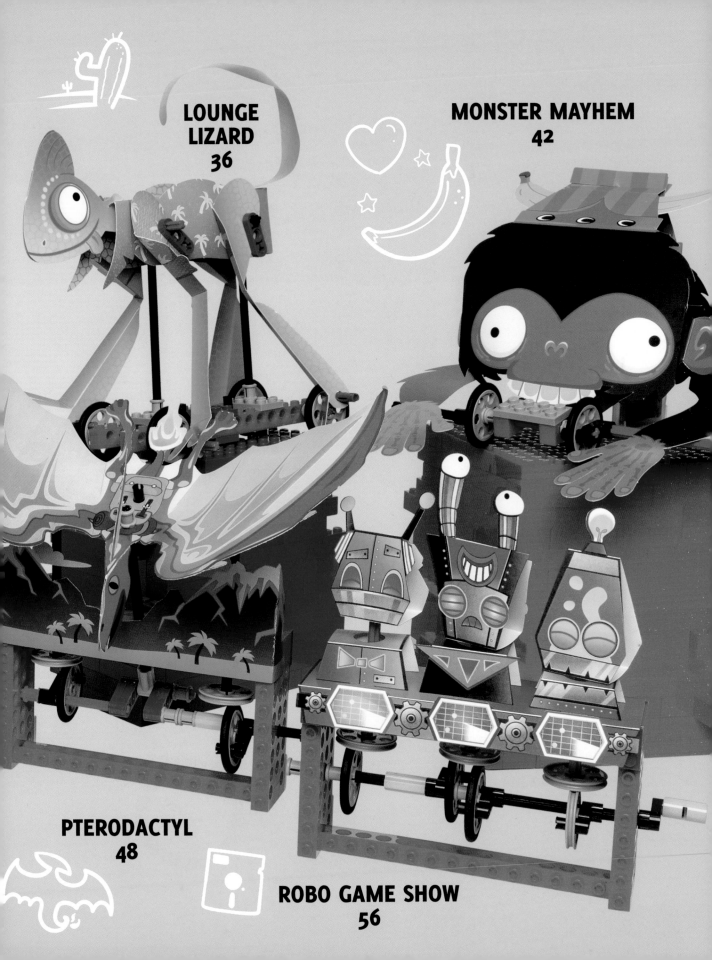

WHAT YOU GET

Get to know the terms used in this book to help you follow the project instructions more efficiently.

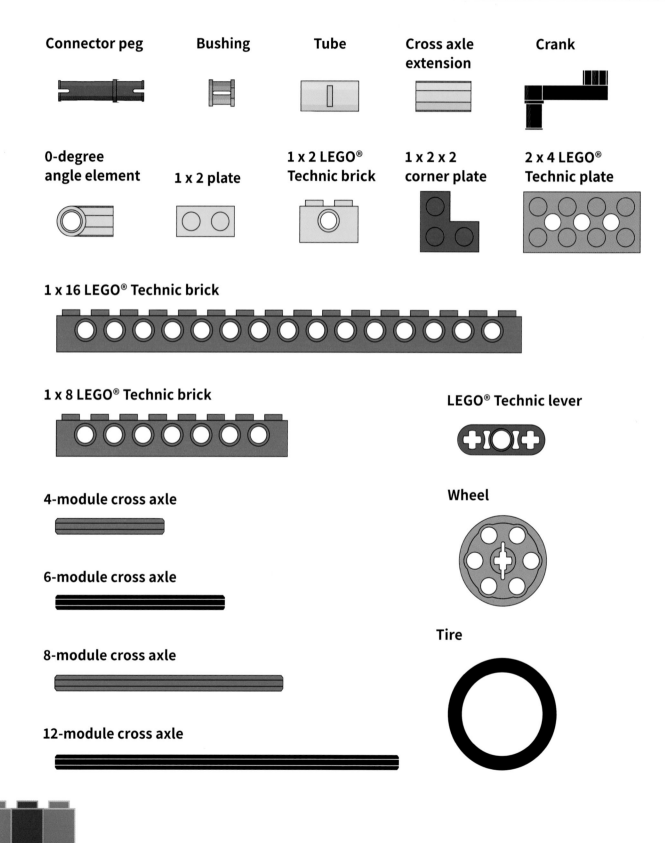

Connector peg

Bushing

Tube

Cross axle extension

Crank

0-degree angle element

1 x 2 plate

1 x 2 LEGO® Technic brick

1 x 2 x 2 corner plate

2 x 4 LEGO® Technic plate

1 x 16 LEGO® Technic brick

1 x 8 LEGO® Technic brick

LEGO® Technic lever

4-module cross axle

Wheel

6-module cross axle

8-module cross axle

Tire

12-module cross axle

A BRIEF INTRODUCTION

Gear Bots are magical, moving mechanisms made from LEGO elements and paper. They are also known as **automata**, or machines that seem to move on their own. People have been making automata for centuries, all around the world. Sometimes automata have been used to solve complex computational problems. Other times, they are wacky art projects designed to make you smile. We like both approaches, but this kit focuses on making the second type.

Factory robots in action!

Fancy, sophisticated robots rely on the same mechanical concepts as Gear Bots. Moving department store window displays (like the kind you might see around Christmas) are the same idea. So are **animatronic animals** (or aliens or monsters) in movies that use practical effects.

Initiate Gear Bot protocol!

GENERAL TIPS & TRICKS

● I box of bricks = 8 projects! You'll need to break down the first model before you build the next one.

● Try taking things apart and building a different way. What happens if you offset a gear? Or replace a crank with a cam?

● The paper characters are perfect for customization. Try gluing or taping materials from home to the paper.

BASIC BOT ANATOMY

- **Shaft** = the horizontal axle, where the "guts" of the Gear Bot go

- **Handle** = the part you turn to get your Gear Bot going

- **Bearing** = the hole that supports the shafts and axles

- **Cam** = a disc that turns on the shaft

- **Crank** = an angular U shape that lifts an axle

Shaft

Bearing

Cam

Crank

Handle

- **Eccentric (ek-SEN-trik)** cams have an off-center placement. Here's how to make the Gear Bots version:

1 Fit the wheel into the rubber tire.

2 Make sure that the central cross-shaped holes match up as you connect the crank to the tire.

3 Your cam is ready for building.

The mechanism that looks like an angular U is called a **crank**. Cranks convert rotating motion (the horizontal axle) into up-and-down motion (the vertical axle.) Your LEGO-built cranks work a lot like pistons in an engine. A typical car engine has four or six cylinders, each with a piston that pumps up and down.

FREQUENTLY ASKED QUESTIONS

Are Gear Bots robots?

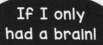

If I only had a brain!

Not exactly. A robot is a machine that does what a computer program tells it to do. However, really, really old automatons were incredibly complex and some people say they were the precursors to computer programming.

Do I have to use the art in the book?

Nope! In fact, we encourage you to put your own spin on the Bots. Maybe you need to cover them in glow-in-the-dark paint or make tin-foil armor. Ordinary craft glue works great for sticking craft supplies to paper.

I love the Gear Bot that I made, and I don't want to take it apart!

We understand. They're pretty great. That's why all the paper parts are easy to remove. You can carefully disassemble the papercraft, and store it in your box for future adventures.

Also, it's a great idea to take photos and videos of your Gear Bots in action.

Of course, you may be able to find similar enough pieces in your own LEGO collection to build your own mechanisms. In which case, you could have an army of Gear Bots at your disposal!

HELI-CACT-ER

Get ready for liftoff as the cactus blossom spins!

YOU WILL NEED

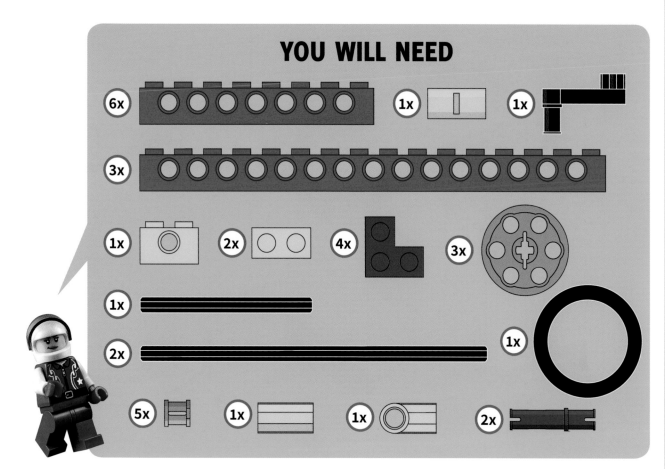

6x

1x

1x

3x

1x

2x

4x

3x

1x

2x

1x

5x

1x

1x

2x

BUILD THE FRAME

1 Add two 1 x 2 x 2 corner plates to the bottom of a 1 x 16 brick.

2 Place a yellow 1 x 2 plate on the bottom of a 1 x 8 brick. Repeat, and add them to the corners.

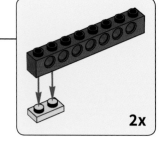

2x

3 Stack a 1 x 16 brick to make a frame.

4 Cap the end of a 6-module cross axle with a bushing.

5 Slide the cross axle through the 1 x 8 brick.

6 Add three bushings.

These **bushings** prevent the axle from shifting sideways.

7 Attach a yellow cross extension and a 12-module cross axle.

8 Add a bushing.

9 Add a wheel with a tire.

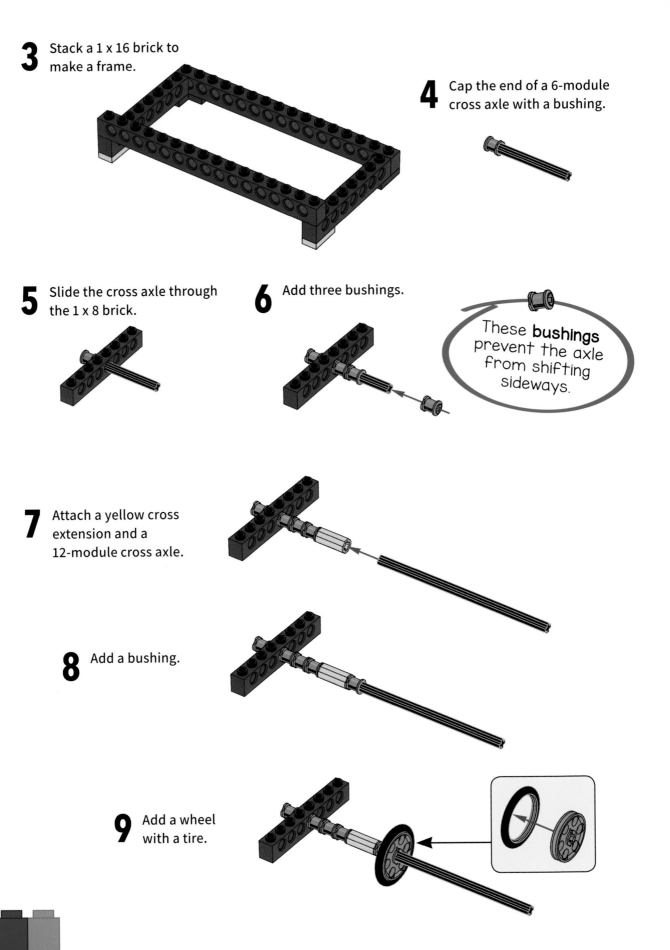

10 Snap the 1 x 8 brick to the frame. Attach another 1 x 8 brick, then add a crank with a tube.

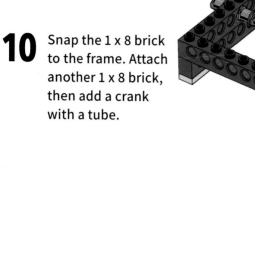

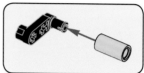

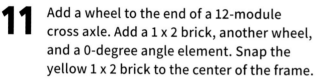

11 Add a wheel to the end of a 12-module cross axle. Add a 1 x 2 brick, another wheel, and a 0-degree angle element. Snap the yellow 1 x 2 brick to the center of the frame.

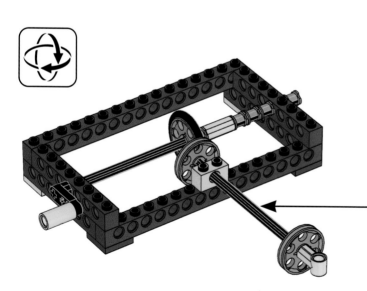

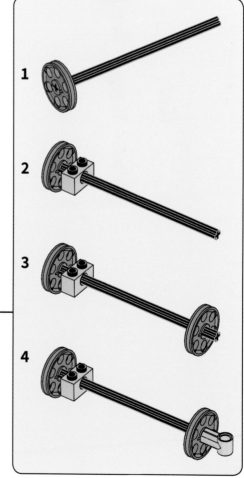

1

2

3

4

TROUBLESHOOTING

The mechanism in the middle of the frame is known as a **friction drive cam**, which creates spinning motion. Once you've built the model, try these experiments. (Find the answers at the bottom of the page.)

1. Try taking the tire off the wheel. Does the heli-cact-er spin faster, slower, or the same? Why do you think that is?

Add pom-poms!

1) Take off this tire.

2) Move this wheel.

2. Then try scooting the cam (the wheel strung on the lower axle) so it touches the right side of the cam follower (the wheel that pushes the axle up and down). What happens to the spinning flower?

1) Slower. The rubber tire creates more friction. 2) The flower spins in the opposite direction!

12 Add a 1 x 16 brick across the yellow 1 x 2 brick. Add two more 1 x 8 bricks to the sides.

13 Add two pegs with friction to the frame, on either side of the 1 x 2 yellow brick.

14 Add two 1 x 2 x 2 corner plates.

PAPER CRAFT

1 Lay the Heli-cact-er facedown and fold up the two middle small tabs.

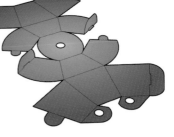

2 Fold the first set of tabs together.

3 Fold the second set of tabs together.

4 Fold the small tabs down and set aside.

5 Remove the wheel, and a 0-degree angle element from the vertical cross axle. Place the cactus feet on the cross axle and blue pegs.

6 Place the assembled cactus on the cross axle and blue pegs with friction.

7 Place the wheel back on the cross axle. Then add the three propellers. Then lock them in place with the 0-degree angle element.

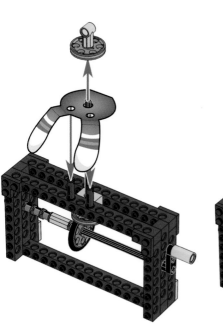

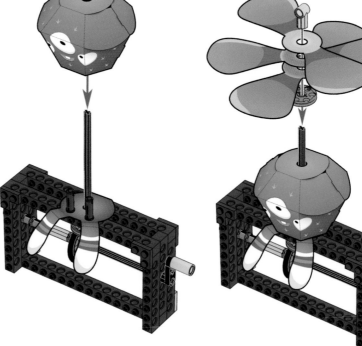

YOU WILL NEED

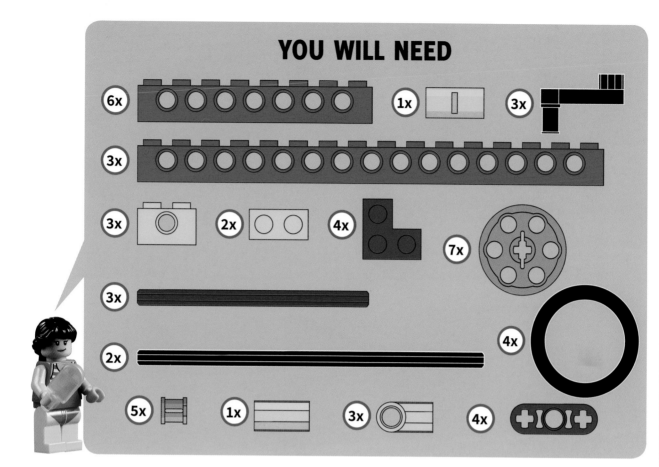

6x 〇〇〇〇〇〇〇 1x [|] 3x

3x 〇〇〇〇〇〇〇〇〇〇〇〇〇〇〇

3x 2x 4x 7x

3x 4x

2x

5x 1x 3x 4x

BUILD THE FRAME

1 Add two 1 x 2 x 2 corners to the bottom of a 1 x 16 brick.

2 Place a yellow 1 x 2 plate on the bottom of a 1 x 8 brick. Repeat, and add them to the corners.

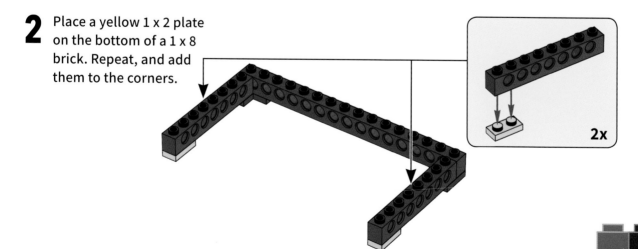

2x

3 Stack a 1 x 16 brick to make a frame. Add a 1 x 8 brick to the left side.

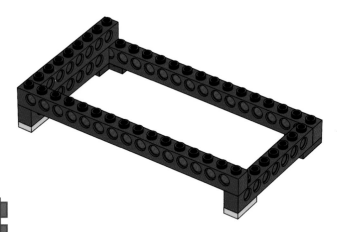

BUILD THE CAMS

4 Add a yellow extension to the end of an 8-module cross axle.

5 Connect a crank to a wheel with a tire. Then add them to the cross axle. Slide a bushing onto the cross axle.

1

2

3

6 Add a wheel with a tire.

7 Slide 3 bushings onto the axle.

8 Add a 12-module cross axle to the yellow extension.

← centered
← eccentric

The left cam is centered. The right cam is **eccentric**. Eccentric cams push automata in interesting ways.

1

2

3

9 Add a crank to a wheel with a tire. Slide them onto the cross axle.

10 Add a wheel with a tire to the cross axle. Add a bushing.

These cams move the DJ back and forth.

Check your work against the picture.

These cams spin the records.

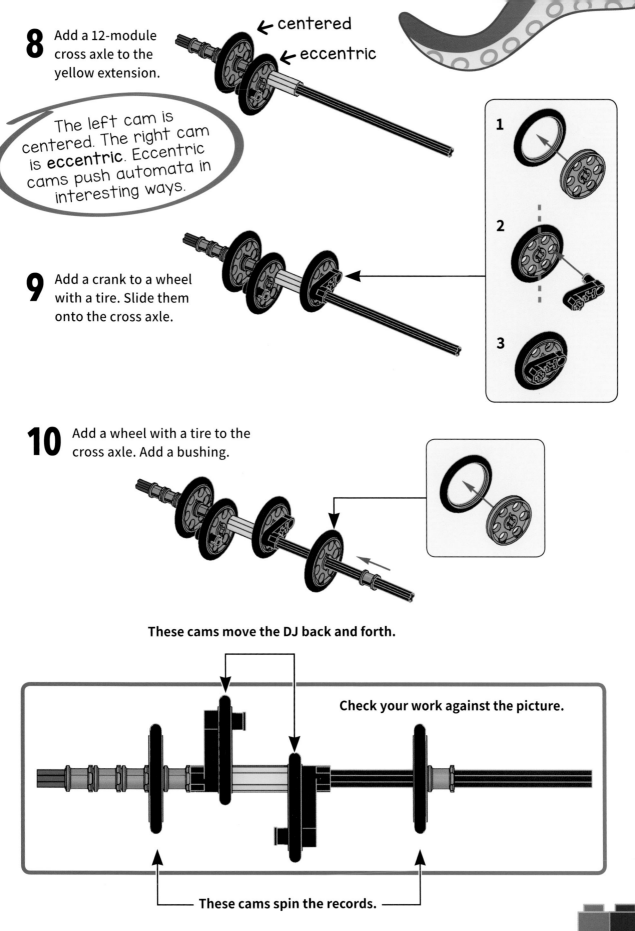

11 Slide a 1 x 8 brick onto the cross axle.

12 Attach the brick to the frame. Make sure the red cross axle goes through the hole on the left.

13 Add a crank with a tube to the cross axle.

CAM FOLLOWERS

14 Place a wheel on the end of an 8-module cross axle. Add a 1 x 2 brick, a lever, and a 0-degree angle element. Build two and snap the 1 x 2 bricks to the frame.

1

2

3

4

2x

15 Build another cam follower, this time using a 12-module cross axle and two levers. Snap the 1 x 2 brick in between the others.

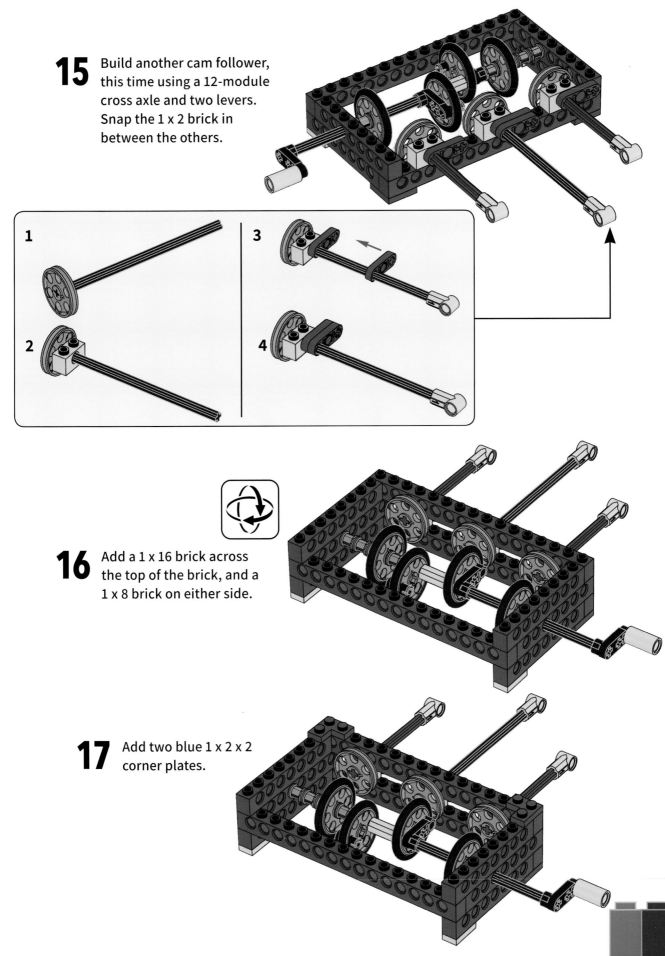

1

2

3

4

16 Add a 1 x 16 brick across the top of the brick, and a 1 x 8 brick on either side.

17 Add two blue 1 x 2 x 2 corner plates.

PAPER CRAFT

1 Lay DJ Bubbles facedown and fold up the five skinny tabs.

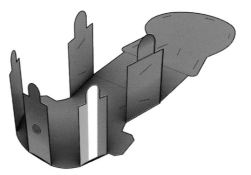

2 Fold the two sides together, slotting the skinny tabs into the slots on the back.

3 Slot the legs into the body of DJ Bubbles.

4 Remove the four blue levers and the three yellow 0-degree angle elements. Fold down the front of the DJ station and slide it over the three cross axles.

Gently press the red axles down until the cam follower wheels rest on the cam tires.

5 Place two of the blue levers over the two red cross axles. Place the two records over the two red cross axles. Replace the two yellow 0-degree angle elements.

6 Place the two blue levers over the black cross axle. Place DJ Bubbles over the black cross axle. Replace the yellow 0-degree angle element.

YETI

THIS SNOW MONSTER IS SPOILING FOR A FIGHT. ITS ARMS MOVE ON CRANKS, WHILE THE BEANIE LIFTS ON AN ECCENTRIC CAM.

YOU WILL NEED

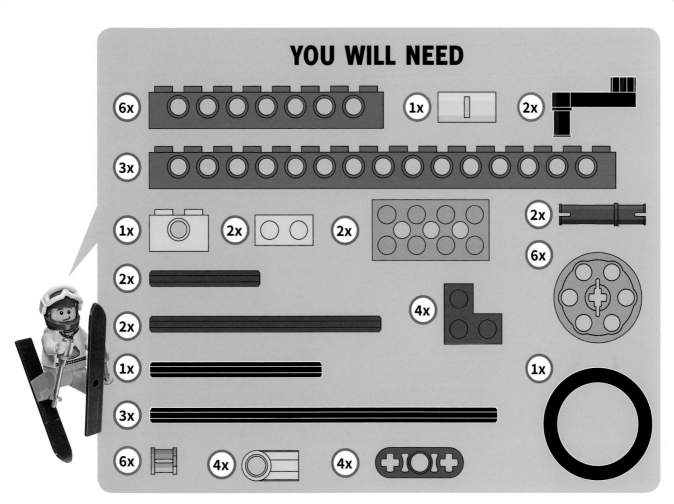

6x (9-module brick)
1x
2x

3x (15-module brick)

1x 2x 2x 2x 2x 6x

4x

2x
2x 1x
1x

3x

6x 4x 4x

BUILD THE FRAME

1 Follow Steps 1–3 of Heli-cact-er to make the frame (pages 9–10).

2 Place a lever at the end of an 8-module cross axle.

3 Add two wheels.

4 Slide a 1 x 8 brick over the cross axle.

23

5 Add a crank with a
tube to the cross axle.

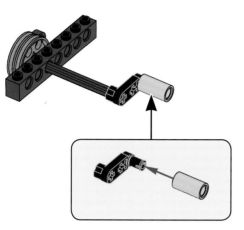

6 Push a 4-module cross axle
into the lever.

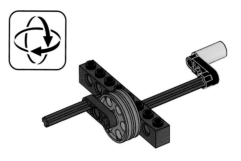

7 Place a 0-degree angle element on either end
of a 12-module cross axle. Push one connector
peg through one end, then attach the other
end to the red cross axle.

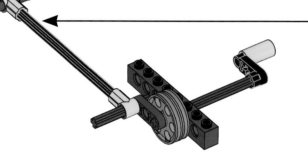

1

2

3

8 Add a bushing and
another lever to the
red cross axle.

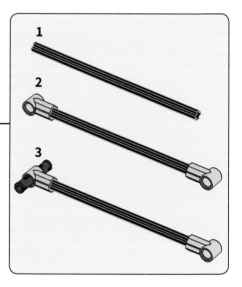

9 Cap the end of an 8-module cross axle with a bushing. Add a lever, another bushing, and finally a crank connected to a wheel with a tire.

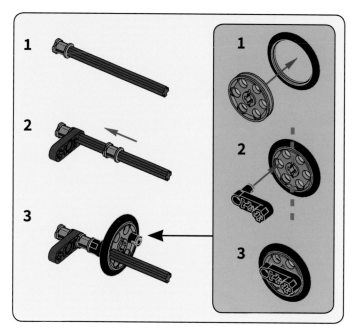

10 Add the cross axle to the lever.

Cross axle from Step 9

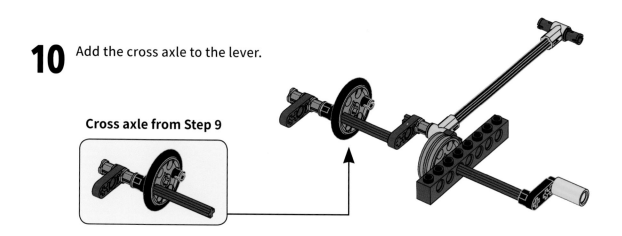

11 Place a lever at the end of a 6-module cross axle.

12 Add two wheels.

13 Add a 4-module cross axle to the lever.

14 Repeat Step 7 to add another liftarm to the red axle.

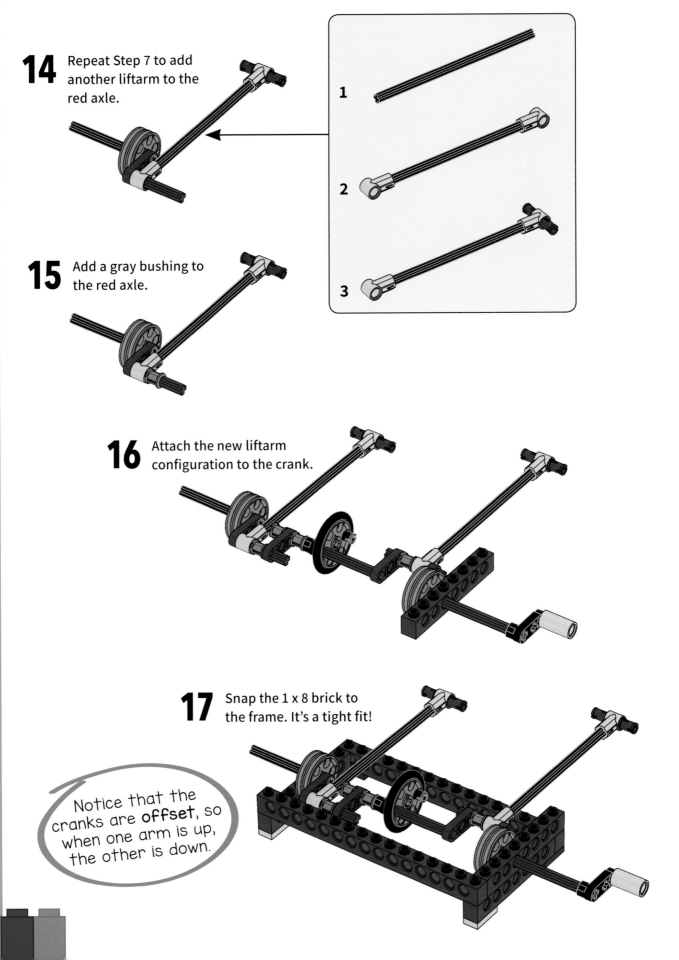

1

2

3

15 Add a gray bushing to the red axle.

16 Attach the new liftarm configuration to the crank.

17 Snap the 1 x 8 brick to the frame. It's a tight fit!

Notice that the cranks are **offset**, so when one arm is up, the other is down.

18 Add another 1 x 8 brick, sliding the cross axle through.

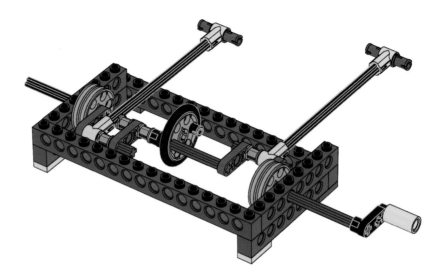

19 Attach a 12-module cross axle to a wheel. Add a 1 x 2 brick and two bushings. Attach the brick to the top of the frame.

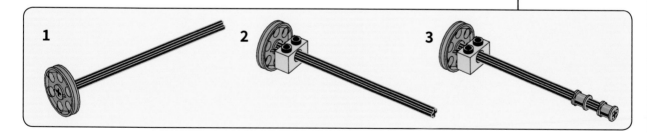

1

2

3

20 Add another 1 x 16 brick, two 1 x 8 bricks, and blue corner plates to complete the frame.

21 Add a 2 x 4 gray plate to the front and back of the frame.

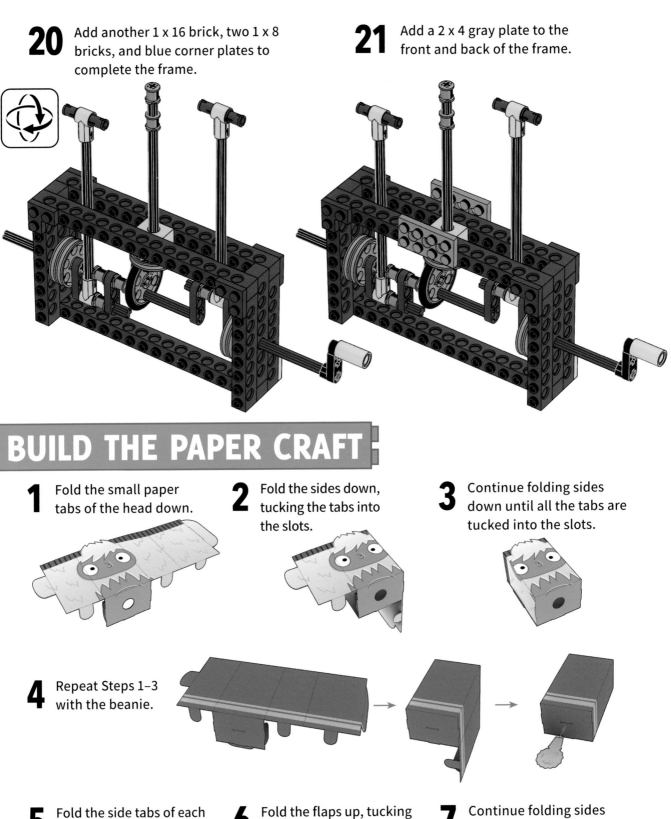

BUILD THE PAPER CRAFT

1 Fold the small paper tabs of the head down.

2 Fold the sides down, tucking the tabs into the slots.

3 Continue folding sides down until all the tabs are tucked into the slots.

4 Repeat Steps 1–3 with the beanie.

5 Fold the side tabs of each arm up.

6 Fold the flaps up, tucking the tabs into the slots.

7 Continue folding sides down until all the tabs are tucked into the slots.

Repeat for the other arm.

8 Place the assembled Yeti face over the center cross axle.

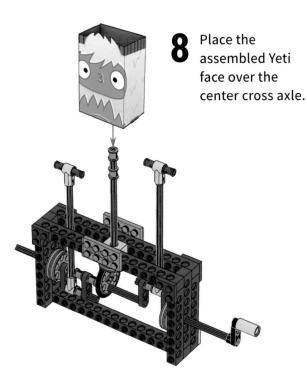

9 Place the assembled Yeti beanie into the Yeti face and over the center cross axle.

10 Slide the arms over the side cross axle assemblies. The blue pegs with friction fit through the holes in the fists.

11 Slip the slot in the end of the arms over the cross axle. The end of the arms should fit into the slot between the top two bricks. If you need to, pop the pegs out and then back in through the fist hole.

HEAD BANGER

Stop hitting yourself . . .

Stop hitting yourself . . .

What goes up, doesn't always go down... If your Head Banger is freezing up, **try placing a small coin** (like a dime or penny) inside the paper fists, to help weigh down the hands.

YOU WILL NEED

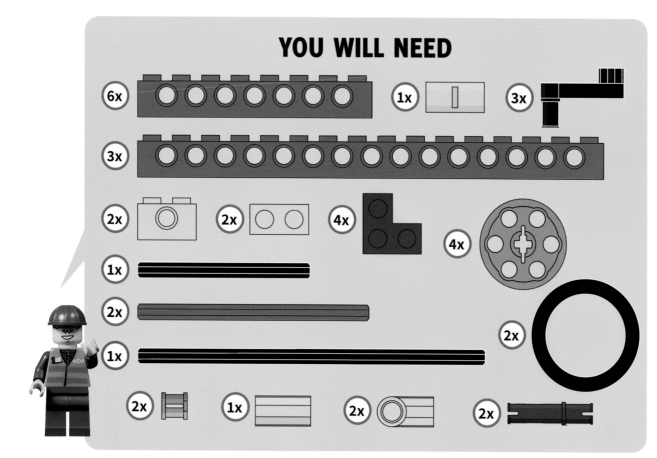

6x
3x
1x
3x
2x 2x 4x 4x
1x
2x 2x
1x
2x 1x 2x 2x

BUILD THE FRAME

1 Follow Steps 1–3 of Heli-cact-er to build the frame (pages 9–10).

2 Add a bushing to the end of a 6-module cross axle.

3 Slide the cross axle into the 1 x 8 brick.
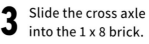

4 Attach a crank to a tire with a wheel, and slide it onto the cross axle.

1   2   3

5 Add a bushing.

6 Add a yellow extension and a 12-module cross axle.

7 Assemble another crank to a tire with a wheel, and add it toward the end of the cross axle.

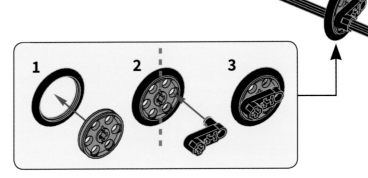

1   2   3

8 Snap the 1 x 8 brick to the frame.

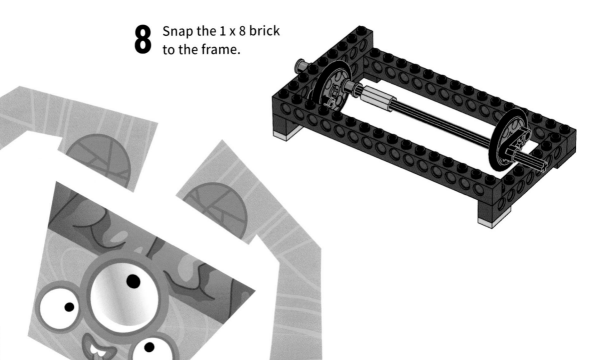

9 Add another 1 x 8 brick, making sure the cross axle goes through. Attach a crank with a tube to the cross axle.

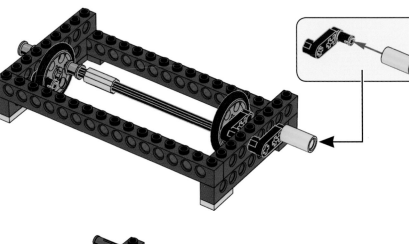

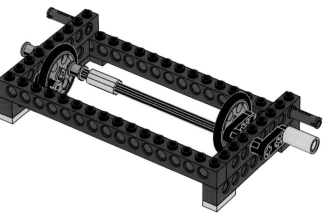

10 Add a connect peg to the left and right sides of the frame.

11 Place a wheel on the end of an 8-module cross axle. Add a 1 x 2 brick and a 0-degree angle element. Build two and snap the 1 x 2 bricks to the frame.

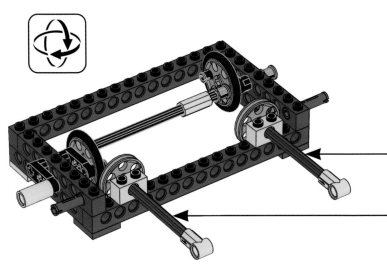

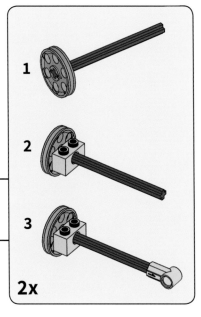

1

2

3

2x

12 Add a 1 x 16 brick, two 1 x 8 bricks, and two corner plates to complete the frame.

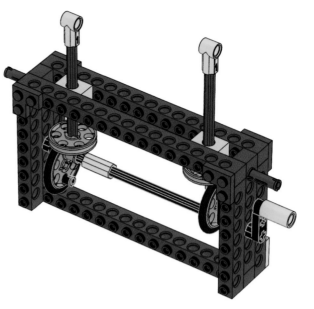

BUILD THE PAPER CRAFT

1 Fold the small paper tabs of the head down.

2 Fold the sides down, tucking the tabs into the slots.

3 Continue folding the sides down until all the the tabs are tucked into the slots.

4 Place each arm with the orange side up. Fold up all the tabs.

5 Fold the fist up.

6 Fold the last two creases and tuck the tabs into the slots.

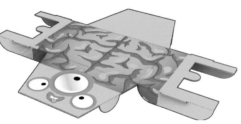

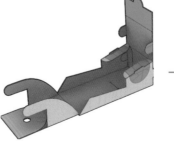

7 Bend the arms back and forth a couple times at the elbow. They should be good and loose.

8 Place the head onto the top of the frame. There should be 3 studs visible on either side. Pop the arms over the two blue pegs on the sides.

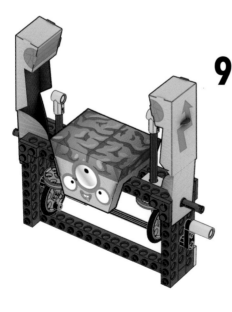

9 Fold the arms in so that the paper hooks fit into the slots in the top of the frame. Rest the fists on top of the two 0-degree angle elements.

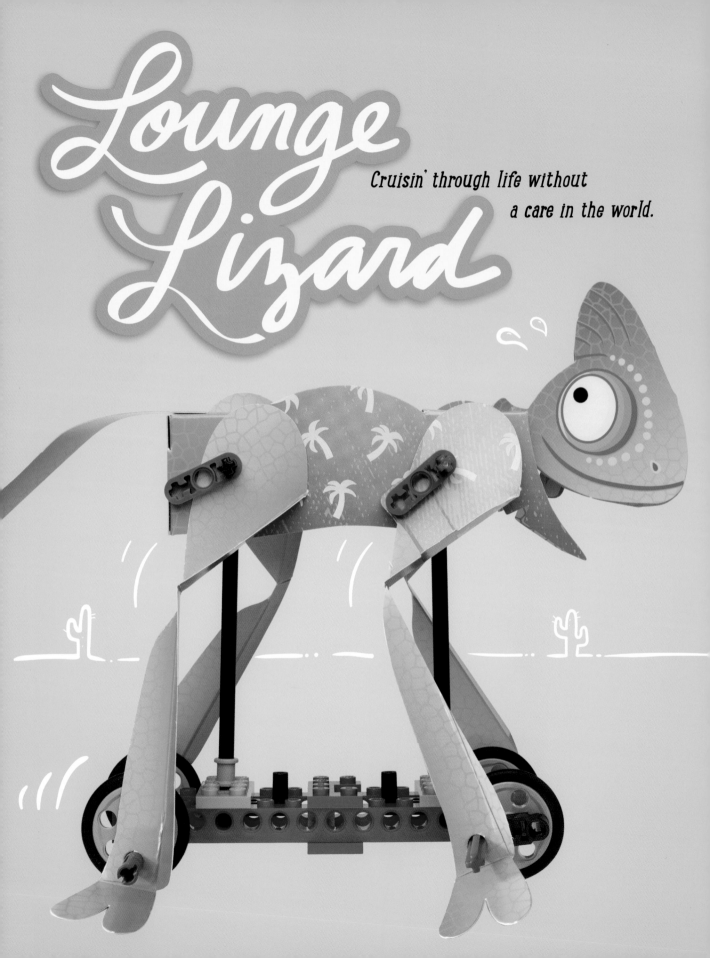

Lounge Lizard

Cruisin' through life without a care in the world.

YOU WILL NEED

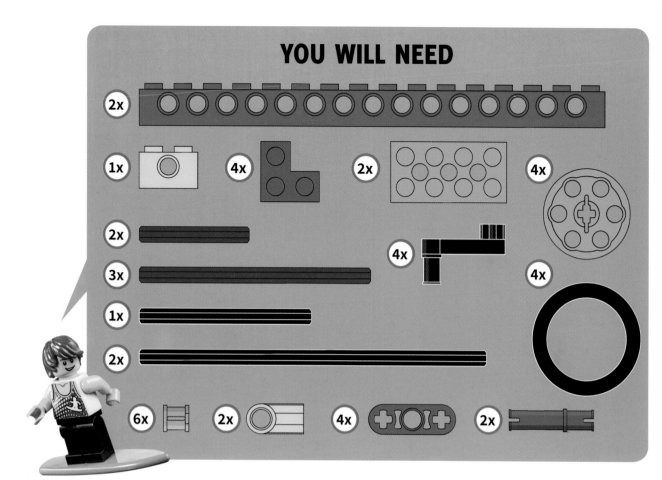

2x
1x 4x 2x 4x
2x
3x
1x 4x 4x
2x
6x 2x 4x 2x

BUILD THE FRAME

1 Connect two blue 1 x 2 x 2 corner plates with a 1 x 2 brick.

2 Place a 1 x 16 brick on either side of the yellow 1 x 2 brick.

3 Lock the red bricks in place with two more blue 1 x 2 x 2 corner plates.

4 Build two posts from a 12-module axle, crank, plate, bushing, and 0-degree angle element. Snap the plates to the red bricks.

1

2

2x

5 Add a 6-module axle and two blue levers to the back post.

6 Then add an 8-module red axle and two blue levers to the front post.

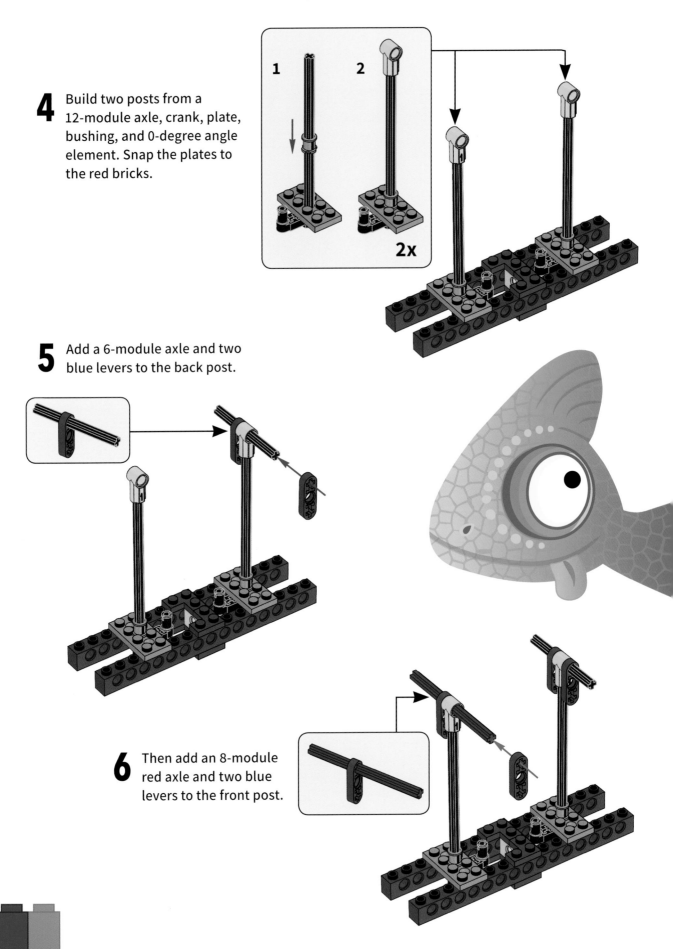

7 Place a bushing on an 8-module red axle, slide it through the holes on the red bricks, and add a bushing to the other end. Repeat on the last set of holes.

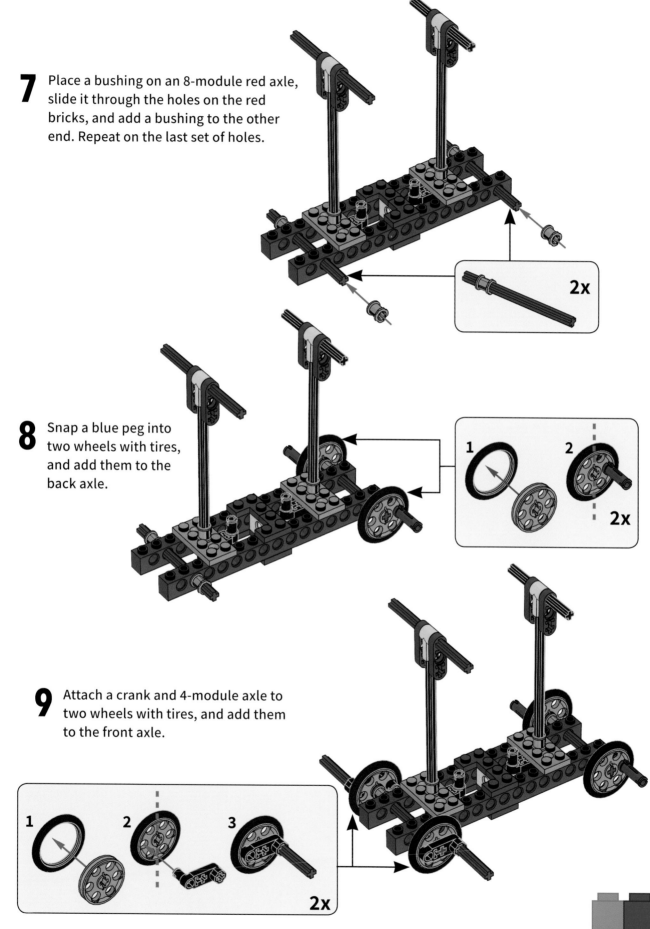

2x

8 Snap a blue peg into two wheels with tires, and add them to the back axle.

1   2   **2x**

9 Attach a crank and 4-module axle to two wheels with tires, and add them to the front axle.

1   2   3   **2x**

1 Start with the Lounge Lizard shirt lying flat.

2 Fold the side flaps down.

3 Fold the bottom flap over. Tuck the tab into the slot.

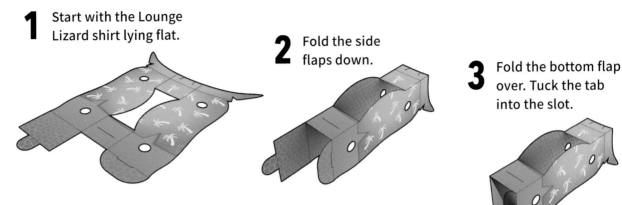

4 Remove the blue levers and cross axles from the top. Place the Lounge Lizard shirt on top and slide the cross axles back in place.

5 Place each hole of the legs over the cross axles and blue pegs. Slide the blue levers back into place to lock it all together.

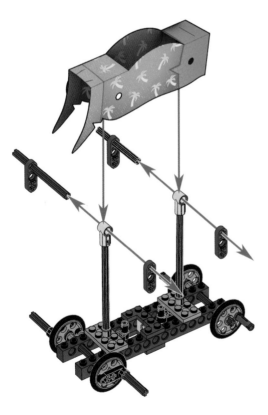

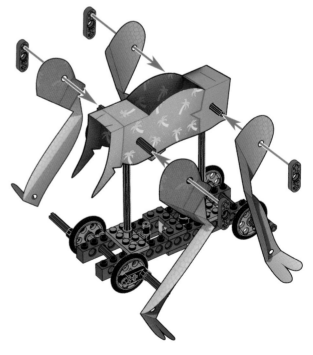

6 Fold the head in half and slot it onto the shirt. Slot the tab on the tail into the slot on the lizard's back.

Up until now you may have only made Gear Bots with handles that turn. An engineer has fancy names for what's going on here. The **input** is the force you apply to the mechanism—usually, it's you, turning the handle. The **output** is what the machine does—a paper character doing something wacky.

Lounge Lizard doesn't have a handle for you to turn . . . so where's the input? Try to think of three different ways you could get your machine to move.

(A FEW IDEAS ARE AT THE BOTTOM OF THE PAGE.)

Some ideas: 1) Push Lounge Lizard with your finger. 2) Tie a string to the front and pull it. 3) Turn on a fan behind Lounge Lizard.

YOU WILL NEED

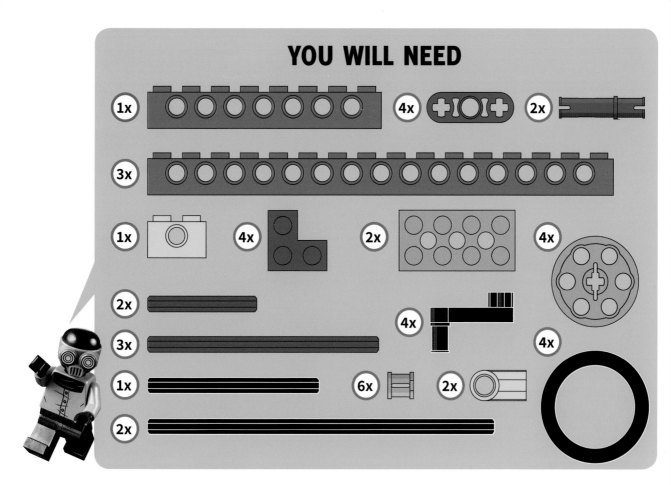

1x
4x
2x

3x

1x
4x
2x
4x

2x
4x

3x
4x

1x
6x
2x

2x

BUILD THE FRAME

1 Connect two blue 1 x 2 x 2 corner plates with a 1 x 2 brick.

2 Place a 1 x 16 brick on either side of the yellow 1 x 2 brick.

3 Snap a gray plate on either end of the frame. Add a bushing to the end of an 8-module red axle, slide it through the first set of holes, and add another bushing. Repeat with the last set of holes.

2x

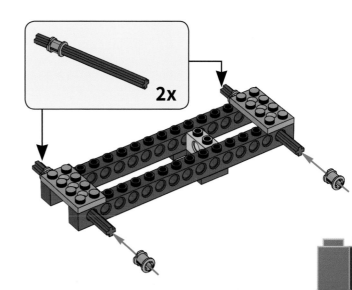

4 Place blue pegs through the first and last holes of a 1 x 16 brick. Add two 1 x 2 x 2 corner plates to the center of the brick, then connect them to a 1 x 8 brick. Add the whole construction to the frame.

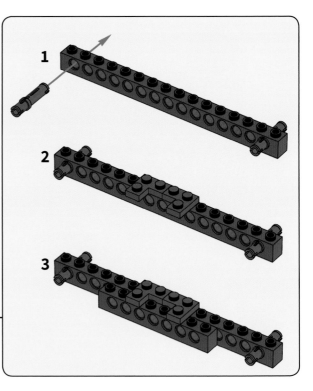

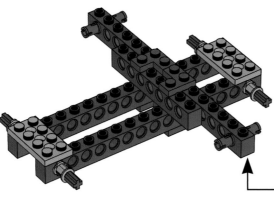

5 Attach a crank and 8-module axle to a wheel with a tire, and thread it through the front axle, nearest you.

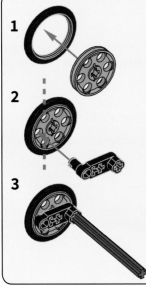

6 Assemble a wheel with a tire, a crank, and a 6-module axle. Then add the wheel to the front axle, farthest from you.

7 Create two spinning poles. Cap the end of a 4-module red axle with a bushing. Then thread a 0-degree angle element with a 12-module cross axle onto the red axle. Assemble a wheel with a tire and crank to the red axle. Attach each pole to the back axle of your car.

8 Add four blue levers to the black spinning poles.

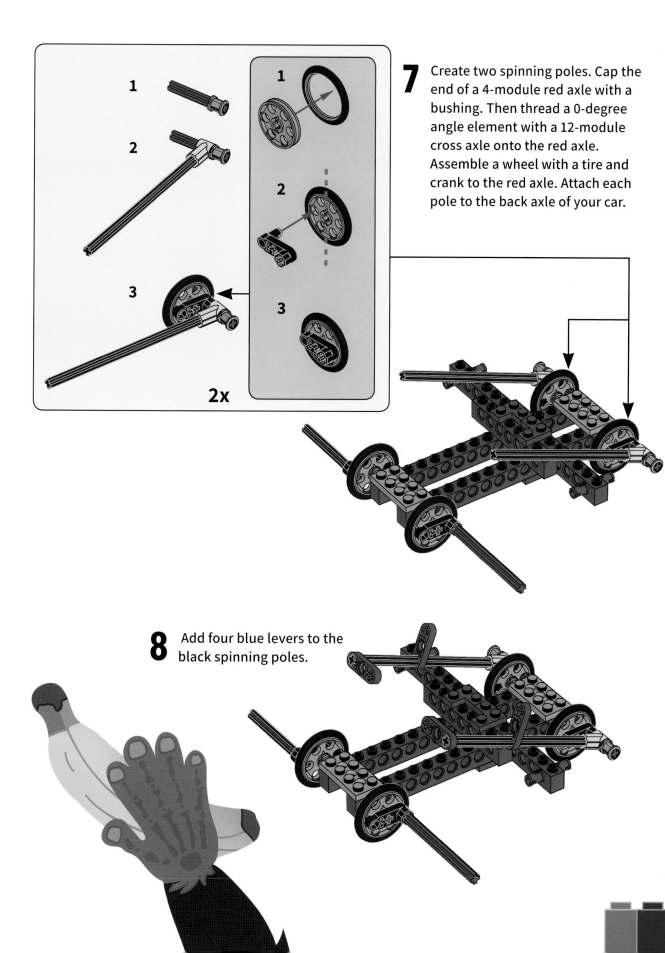

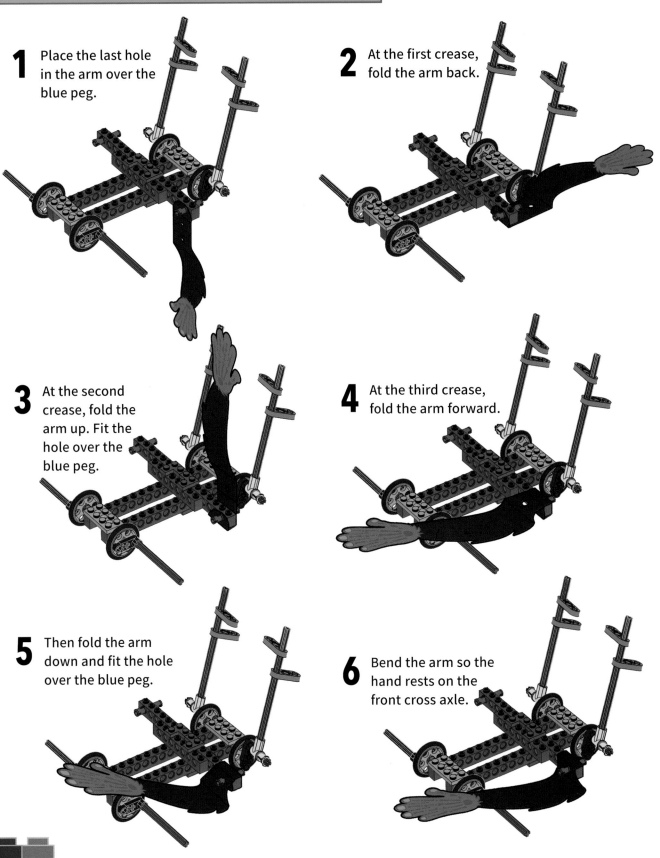

1 Place the last hole in the arm over the blue peg.

2 At the first crease, fold the arm back.

3 At the second crease, fold the arm up. Fit the hole over the blue peg.

4 At the third crease, fold the arm forward.

5 Then fold the arm down and fit the hole over the blue peg.

6 Bend the arm so the hand rests on the front cross axle.

7 Remove the top two levers. Then slide the back of the monster head over the two black spinning poles.

8 Slot the front of the monster head onto the back of the monster head.

9 Fold the front of the monster head down until back tabs slot over the black spinning poles.

10 Add two blue levers to the cross axles to lock the monster head in place. You might need to unslot the green head pieces to reach.

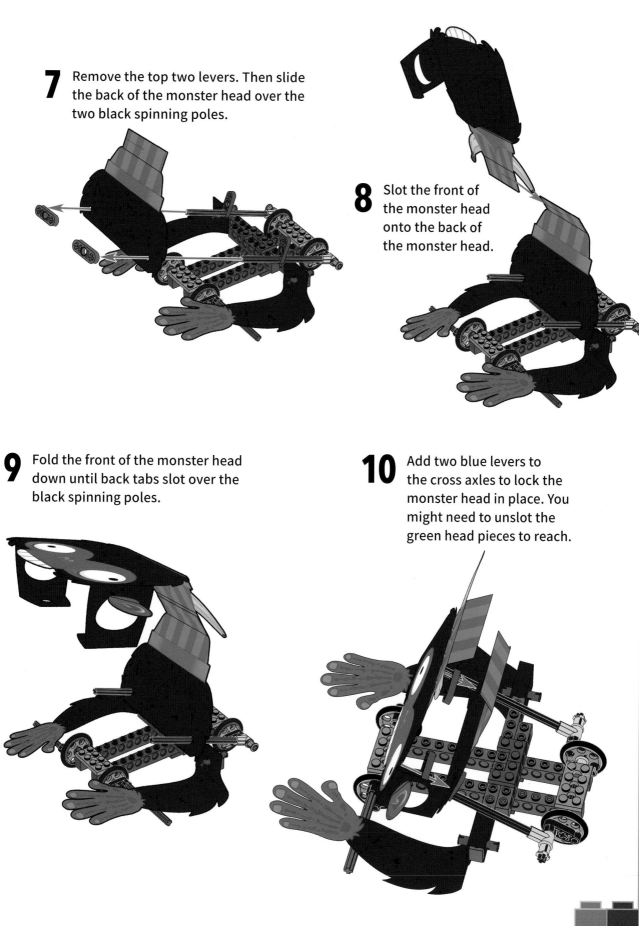

YOU WILL NEED

6x ○○○○○○○
1x ▢
4x ▄▄▄

3x ○○○○○○○○○○○○○○○

2x ▢
2x ○○
4x ◲
4x ⊙
2x ◯

2x ▬
1x ▬▬
1x ▬▬
3x ▬▬▬

6x ▦
1x ▤
3x ◎
4x ✛◉✛

BUILD THE FRAME

1 Follow Steps 1–3 of Heli-cact-er to make a frame (pages 9–10).

2 Attach the 4-module red cross axle to the cross axle extension.

3 Add two bushings to the axle.

4 Then add two blue levers.

5 Slide a 4-module red axle with a bushing through the levers.

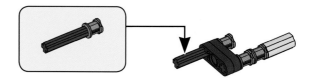

6 Cap a 12-module axle with a yellow 0-degree angle element. Add a crank and bushing to the axle, then slide the yellow element over the red axle.

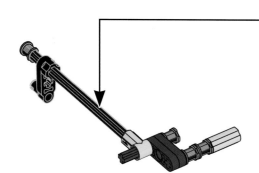

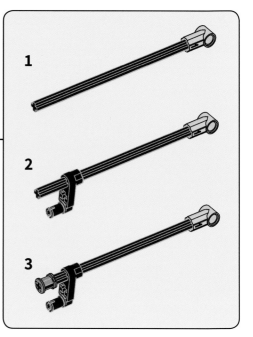

1

2

3

7 Add two blue levers to the red axle.

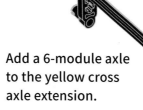

8 Add a 6-module axle to the yellow cross axle extension.

9 Build a wheel with a tire and a crank. Then add it to the black axle.

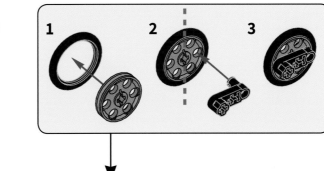

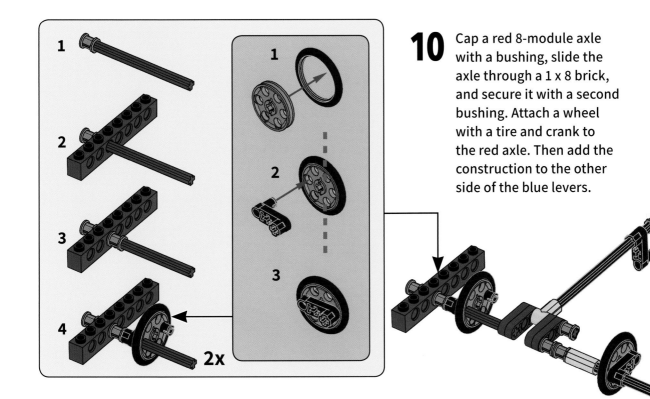

10 Cap a red 8-module axle with a bushing, slide the axle through a 1 x 8 brick, and secure it with a second bushing. Attach a wheel with a tire and crank to the red axle. Then add the construction to the other side of the blue levers.

11 Add the 1 x 8 brick to the frame.

12 Add another 1 x 8 brick over the black axle. Then add a crank with a tube.

13 Assemble two liftarms using a wheel, 12-module axle, 1 x 2 brick, and 0-degree angle element. Snap the bricks to the frame.

1

2

3

2x

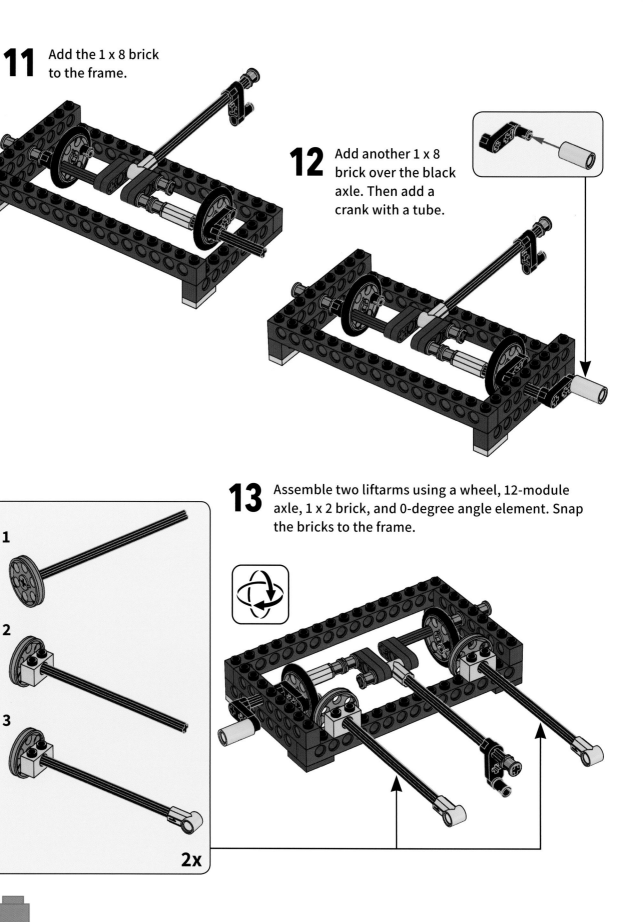

14
Add a 1 x 16 brick and two more 1 x 8 bricks to complete the frame.

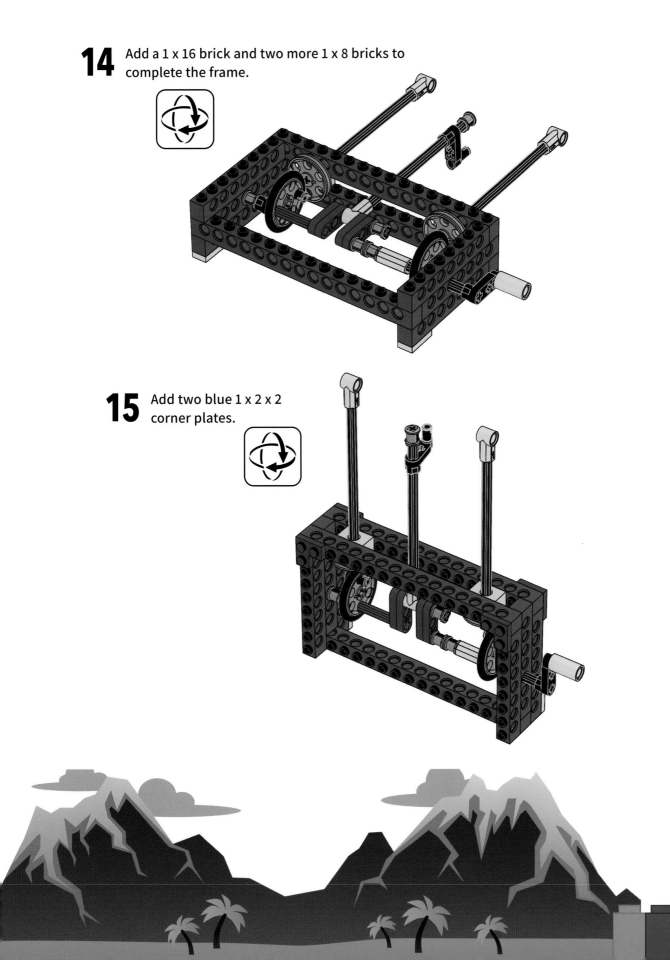

15
Add two blue 1 x 2 x 2 corner plates.

1 Fold the wings back and forth a few times so they can flap easily.

2 Fold the sides of the Pterodactyl's head down.

3 Slot the tab on the crest into the slot in the top of the Pterodactyl's head.

4 Remove the gray bushing from the center cross axle. Place the Pterodactyl over the cross axle and lever. Replace the gray bushing.

5 It's a good idea to fold the wings up and down a couple times to loosen them up so they flap better.

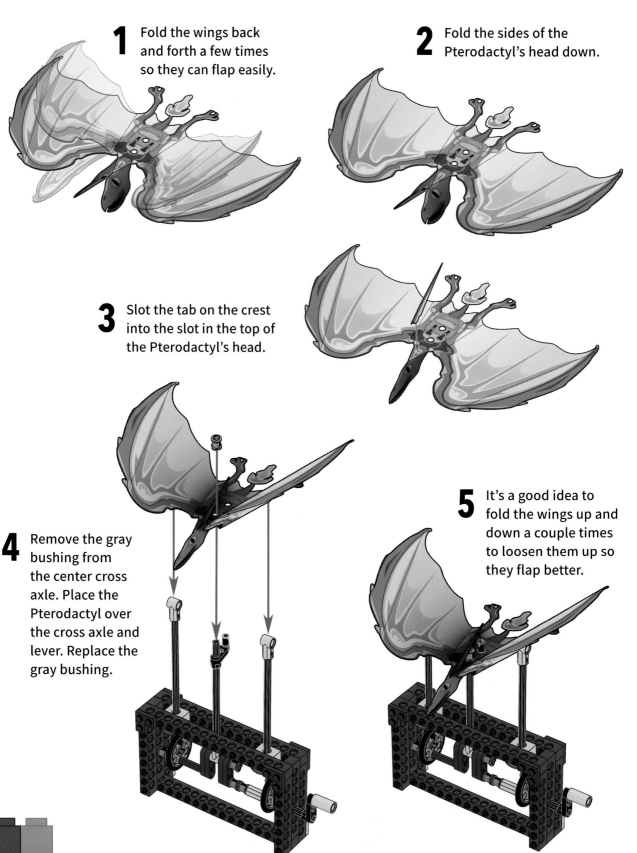

6 Fold the small tabs forward.

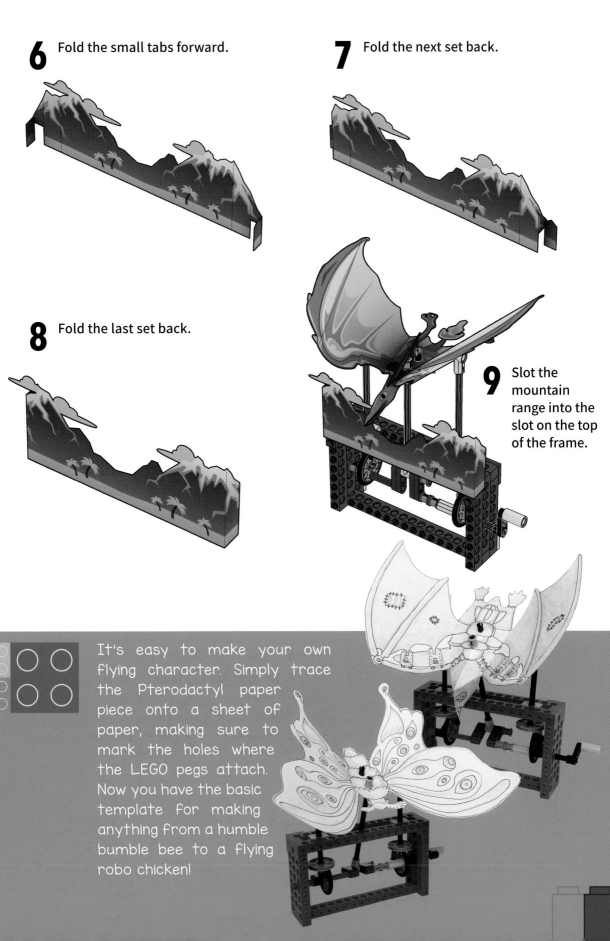

7 Fold the next set back.

8 Fold the last set back.

9 Slot the mountain range into the slot on the top of the frame.

It's easy to make your own flying character. Simply trace the Pterodactyl paper piece onto a sheet of paper, making sure to mark the holes where the LEGO pegs attach. Now you have the basic template for making anything from a humble bumble bee to a flying robo chicken!

YOU WILL NEED

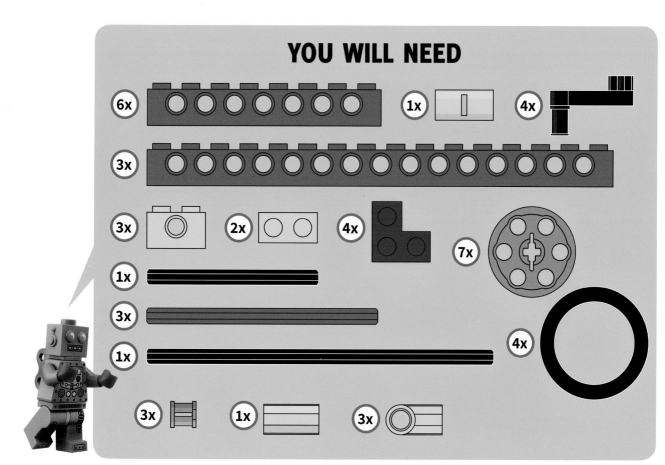

6x **1x** **4x**

3x

3x **2x** **4x** **7x**

1x **4x**

3x

1x

3x **1x** **3x**

BUILD THE FRAME

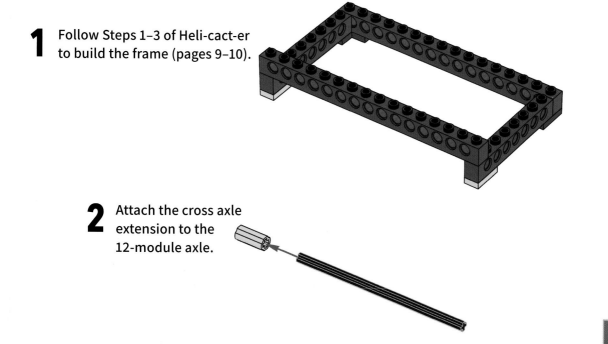

1 Follow Steps 1–3 of Heli-cact-er to build the frame (pages 9–10).

2 Attach the cross axle extension to the 12-module axle.

3 Assemble a wheel with a tire and crank. Slide it onto the axle.

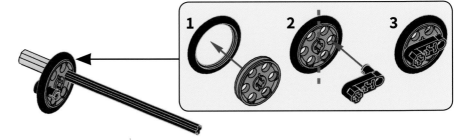

4 Add a bushing.

5 Build two more wheel, tire, and crank constructions, and add them to the axle.

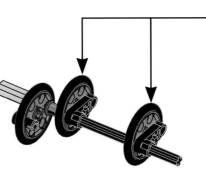

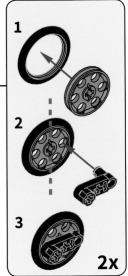

2x

6 Cap a 6-module axle with a bushing.

7 Slide the axle onto a 1 x 8 brick.

8 Add another bushing.

9 Then add a wheel with a tire to the axle.

10 Finally, connect the axle to the yellow cross axle extension.

11 Snap the 1 x 8 brick to the frame.

12 Add another 1 x 8 brick, then connect the axle to a crank with a tube.

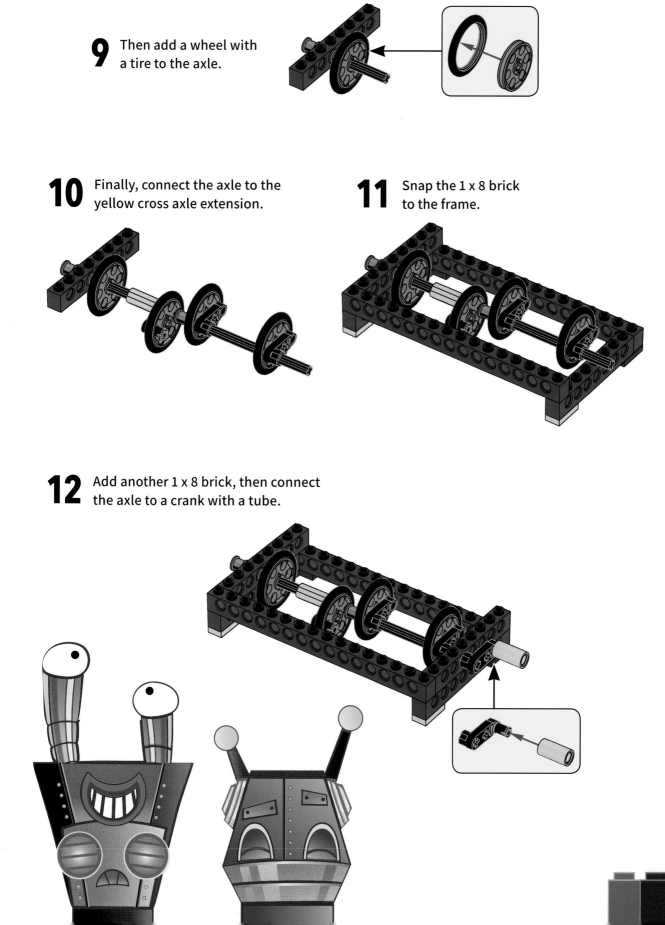

13 Build three cam followers, each with a wheel, 8-module axle, 1 x 2 brick, and 0-degree angle element. Snap the bricks to the frame.

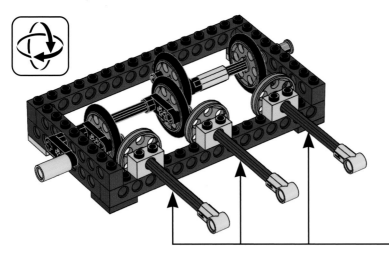

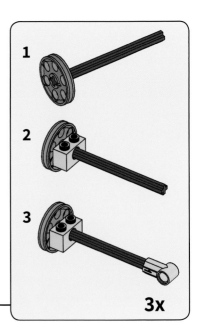

1

2

3

3x

14 Complete the frame with a 1 x 16 brick and two 1 x 8 bricks.

15 Then add two 1 x 2 x 2 corner plates.

BUILD THE PAPER CRAFT

1 Fold the outside flaps on one of the bodies down.

2 Fold the front of the robo platform down. Slot the tabs on the body into the slots on the robo platform.

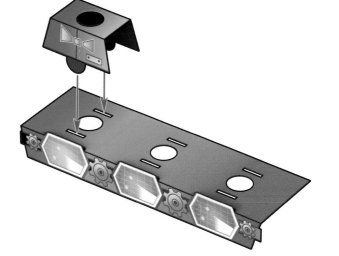

3 Repeat with the other two bodies and place the assembled paper craft onto the frame.

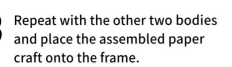

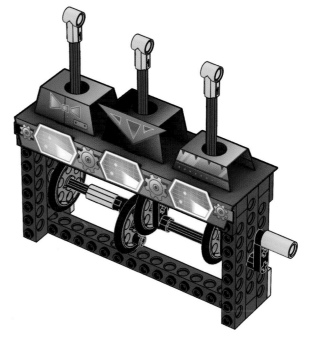

4 Lay one of the robot heads facedown. Fold the two triangular flaps up.

5 Fold the flaps up and tuck them into the slots.

6 Fold the back of the robot head up.

7 Fold the front of the robot head up.

8 Turn the head around, fold the top flap down, and tuck it into the slot.

9 Repeat Steps 4–8 with the other two heads.

10 Place the heads over the red cross axles and yellow 0-degree angle elements.

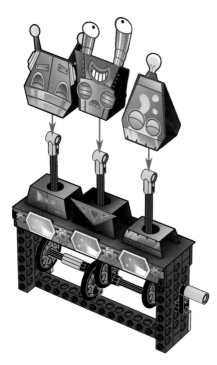

This masterpiece links three different mechanisms that you have learned to build over the course of this book. The red robot nodding "yes" uses one **eccentric cam** to push the axle up and down. Dr. "No" uses two **eccentric cams** to push the axle back and forth. The extremely confused green contestant spins around thanks to the **friction drive cam**. If you study this Gear Bot long enough, you just might unlock the mysteries of the universe.

ARE GEAR BOTS SCIENTIFIC?

They sure are! If you want to dig deeper into the science of Gear Bots, here are some topics you can research:

Automatons

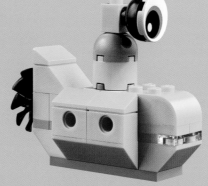

Mechanical engineering

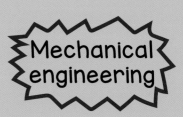

Simple & compound machines

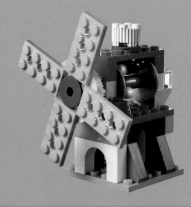

Biomimicry (when machines copy how a living thing moves)